THE MUSEUM of DUBIOUS ART

Collected Drawings

by Neil Baker

authorHOUSE®

AuthorHouse™
1663 Liberty Drive
Bloomington, IN 47403
www.authorhouse.com
Phone: 1-800-839-8640

Published by AuthorHouse 6/18/2013

ISBN: 978-1-4772-8676-0 (sc)
ISBN: 978-1-4772-8675-3 (e)

Library of Congress Control Number: 2012921720

Contents

Introduction

You are about to embark upon a journey in a land of illustrations with a message … multiple messages.

In drawing, my goal is to touch the "child" within all of us. The more humorous the better; however, I do not limit myself to the mere whimsical nature of man, but also attempt to expand my expression into the more serious and somber aspects of existence as well. My style is spontaneous in that I sit down with nothing but a line and the innumerable deviations of such to guide me. Even though my subjects and themes cover a wide variety of topics, my drawings strive for a universal appeal with a bit of social commentary. More often than not my characters will appear off balance, with exaggerated features and proportions, but this is all in an attempt to keep the expression interesting and eye catching. I view my characters as both people and creatures in the world, however distorted. In some form, the following satirical caricatures and scenes should be viewed both as simplistic and challenging.

Please note that according to AuthorHouse's policies, my publishers have removed any depictions of both male and female genitalia from any drawings that contained such visuals. Although the number of these drawings are limited, I, as the artist, apologize for the required discretions.

Beach Couple

Singing The Blues

Graduation Day

The Boss

Park Bench

Te Leus Le Dog

Gay Bar

Jonah

Two Thinking Rabbis

Young Ornithologist

Revolution

The Stone Throwers

The Lost Child

Sophisticated Ladies

Renaissance

The Pursuit

Three Brothers

Life Is Not A Beach

The Stairway

The Evangelist

Circus Preview

Novus Ordo Seclorum

Surprise Visit

First Glance

The Comforting Therapist

Hollywood Mogul

Moonlight Escapade

Mother's Against Abortion

Out The Z Room

Alka-Helter

Boredom

Watchdog

Divorce Court

Hanukkah Cats

Judy Tormenting Demons

Don Decodey

The Other Woman

Custody Battle

Recording Studio

Curtain Call

Quick Dip

Family Outing

Off To Work

Manhunt

Felina's Cat Show

How To Seduce Eve

Basket Cases

Strange Encounter On A Sunday

Civil War Secrets

Confounding The Law

The Death Of Gaia

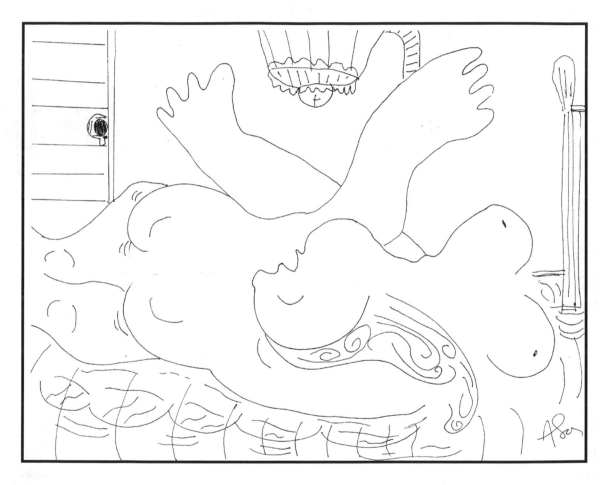

Nude Dreams

I Prefer Someone A Bit More Agressive

Arresting Farmer John

The Boxer's Genie

Cross Dresser

Hen Pecked

Four Masons

The Entomologist

Snail Crossing

Harvey and the Parlor

Mother's Day

Mother's KISS

Real Estate Ladies

Christmas Day

Born to Be Mom's

Satan's Flee

Lost Innocence

Hollywood Premier

The Actor's Assassin

Garage Sale

Mrs. "L"

Rock Star Obsession

Friday Night Boxing

Final Hour

The Nymphs

The Prisoner

The Audition

Chinese Cat

Fisherman's Protest

Venice Ballerinas

Nightclub Thanatos

The Fishers

The Kite Flyer

NRF

Street Scene

Blind Revision

Bit Tipsy

Witch Doctor

Three Muses

No Smoking

Disappearing Act

Pet Food Stand

The Classroom

Same Old Shit

Bathing

King Zeus

E=MC Dog

Pisces

Emergency Ward

Professor Anthropology

Nude Hazing

Dating the Professor

Hypnotic Seduction

Pan's Education

The Long Signal

Disc Jockeys

Bums in the Park

Nude Ink

The Queen Bee

Can You Spare Ten Minutes Of Pure Romance?

Caen and Mabel

Another Sunday In Death Valley

The Rivals

Never Ending Beer

Psychic Fair

War Suckers

Swimming Pool Lessons

Annie Holic

"Too-Much" Lotion

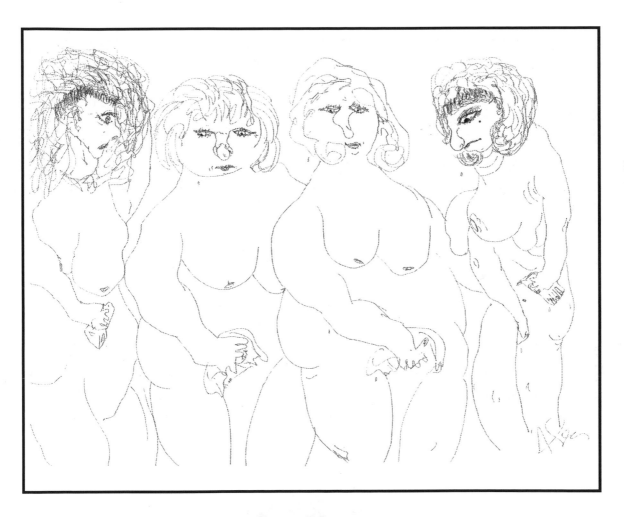

Scrubbing

Three Knitters

Mothers At The Beach

Anything Goes

The Holdup

The Payoff

New Neighbors

The Sculptor

Murder at Motel 6

Peeping Tom

Drug Bust

Tribal Chiefs

Vegetarian Fortune Teller

Sink or Swim

Four Seasons

The Outlaws

Concentration Camp

Family Portrait At The Beach

Picking Daffodils

The Rape

If This Date Doesn't Work Out, Can We Go Dutch?

Buddies

The Affair

Asking Directions

Three Fishermen

RoseEmerald

Delusions

Springtime

Soviet Rabbis

Noah's Ark

Dancing Rabbis

Three Warriors

Birdwatcher

The Museum Of Dubious Art

Looking for Work

Jesus Casting Out Demons

On Grandma's Farm

Act IV, Scene I of "Hercules Goes To The Circus"

Sumo Wrestlers

The Burning Bush

Bar Mitzvah

Disciples

Rings

Peas

Census Taker

The Terrorist

Problem Child

The Bomb Shelter

Bad Influence

The Outcast

Cave Cats

The Argument

Unicycle

Blind Date

The Killing Of Saul At The Battle Of Gilboa

Future Graduates

Mother Hens

The Kid

Orphans

Recess

Poker Chip

Floating Lovers

Aerobic Twins

Waiting At The Elevator

The Kiss

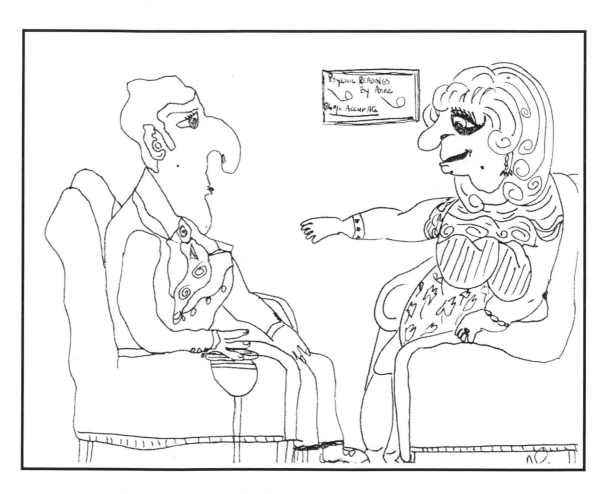

Psychic Readings 86% Accurate

Galileo Faces The Inquisition

Time Warp

The Reader

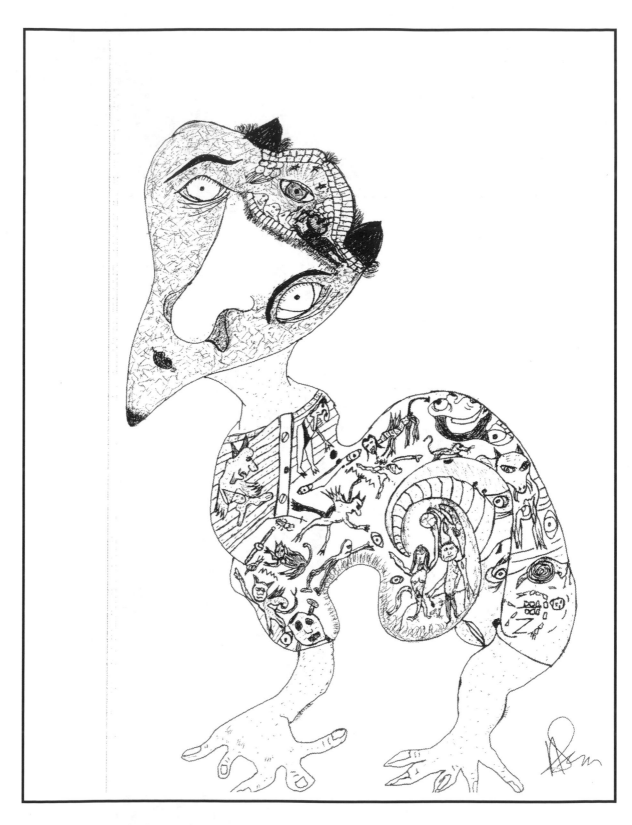

Creature From The Garden Of Eden

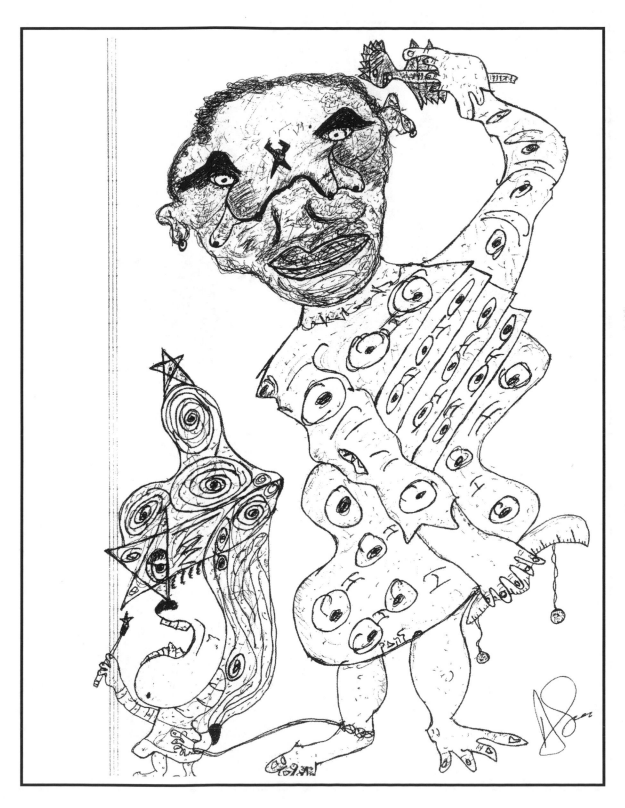

Black Magic

Nazi Fairies

And God Created Eve

Satan and the Jew

Satan on Wheels

Susie's Outing In The Park

Devon And His Mystical Dog

Riverboat Preacher

Homeless Girl

US Marine Corps

Tattoo Cat

Nudist Camp Couple

The Zolohoffs

Xymetria

Twin Kenyans

Eve's Dark Side

Demon Hunters

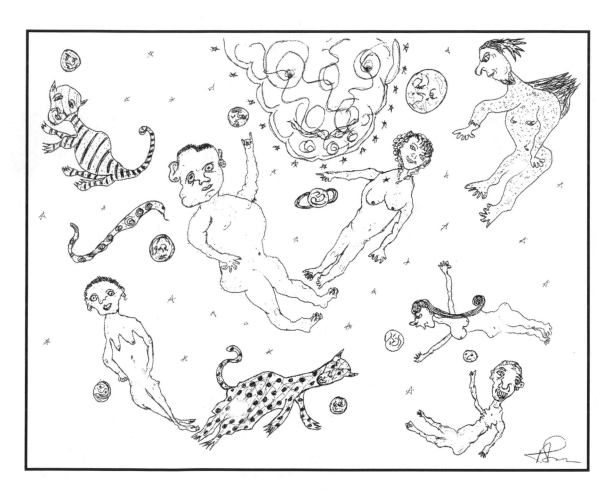

Celestial Forces

The Tarot Reading

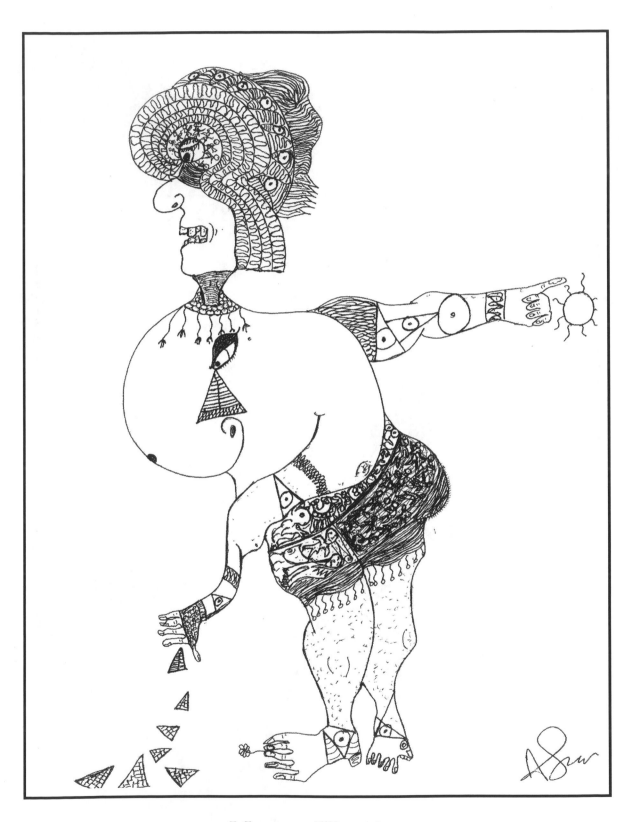

Mayan Warrior

Bolemba from Uranus

Ballet Karate

The Bobecks

Flower's Lament

Cayman's Cat Rat

215

Eight Entities

Mazuma Holding Flower

Demelia Holding Head

Pregnant Curlassa

Uncle Georges

Becoming Brown

City Crosswalk

Longuini And Gelato

Cat In Heaven

Ballet Fairy With Cat

Professor Polinski Walking Kielbasa The Dog

Two Cats And A Dinosaur

Man In Scalene Shirt

Hobos

229

Janek Composing Jamaica Drum Song

The Death Of Centaur

Jogging On The Sabbath

Trotsky Contemplating Life

Peruvian Gypsy

The Sailor

Stromboli And Ape Boy

Miloletta The Mountain Cat

Asmat's Birthday Gift

Teaching Mockingbird

Wildcat

Adam Before Eve

Gay Pride Beehive

Jules The Surfer

Quinto The Pirate

Liza Minelli Walking Her Dog

Exodus From Eden

Naked Zuma

Demons Lounging

Gay Stroll

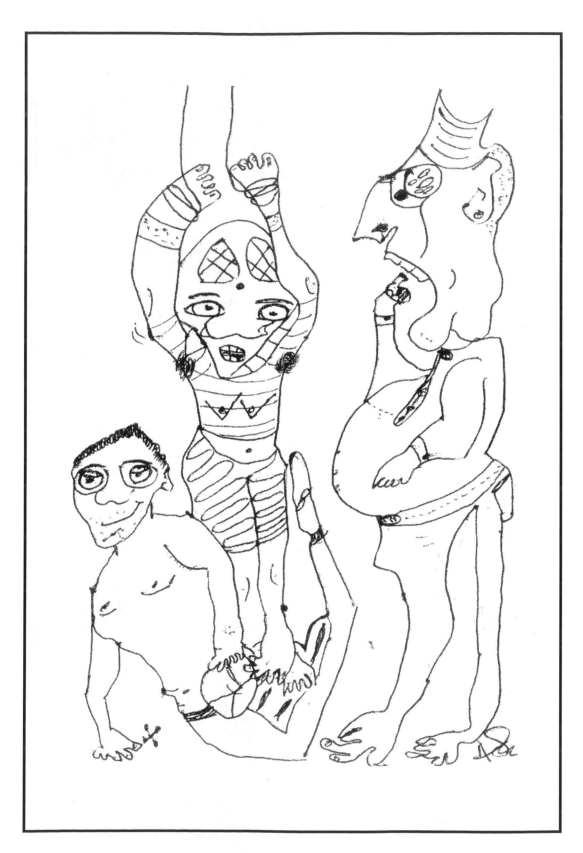

Rude Martian Landing

The Joy Of Acting

Shelmiel In The Desert

Burning Man Fans

Serbian Man and Friend

Adam And Eve After The Fact

Hot Basketball

Bozo And Sambo

Eve Flirting With Argyle

The Francellos

Three Bearded Sons

Three Spirit Sit-Ups

Post Divorce Fishing Trip

Coed Baseball

Big Valentine's Day Head Card

Circus Acts

Shower Line

Lou-Seal

Interviewing Ryan

Cain In Nod

The Joplins

The Florist Brothers

Card Woman

Z Moon

Zippers At Home With Mouse

Crow Woman

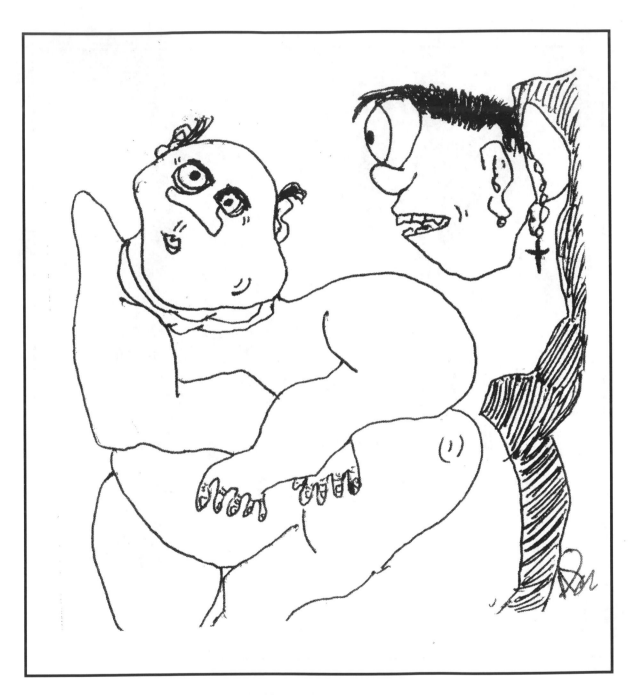

Tess Saddlebag

Mother Decides To Tag Along

End Of Gaydom

Adam And Eve Hiding Genitals

My Pal Satan

Big Headed Man Doing Yoga

Somecata The Gypsy-Man

Man Walking Monk Cat

Sailor In Trouble

Satan's Curtain Call

Beach Combing

Desert Journey

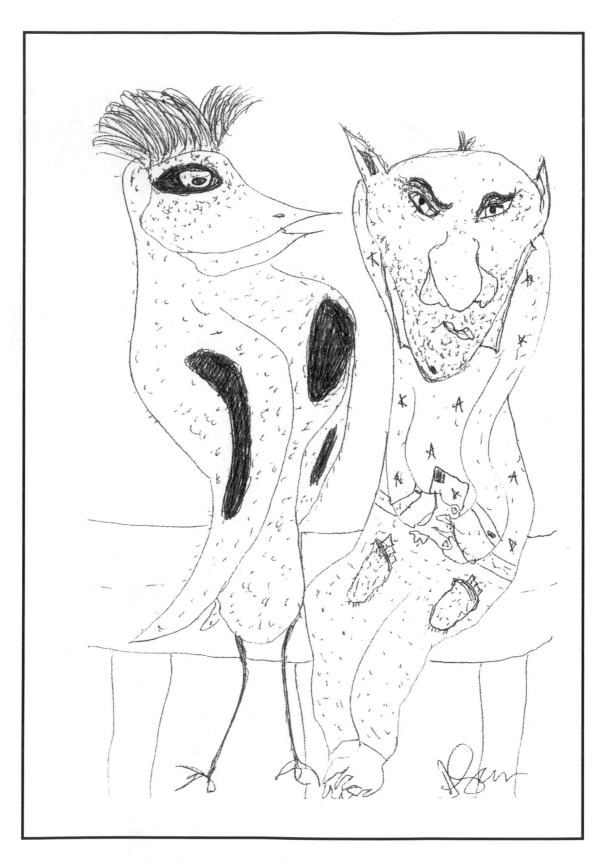

Benched By A Cuckoo Bird

Moonlight Reject

Tom

Their Only Son

Starcat

Kyle's Poodle

Mona Lisa's Day Off

Bad Tarot

Cat's Pete

Kabuki Cat

Wisdom Teeth

My Cat Cat

Lancette and Freud

Eve Being Watched By God

Ellen Phata's Son

Zuma's Head

The Gostofs

Pajama

Leaving Home With Pet 'Peeve'

Leticia

Disney Reject

Man Dreams

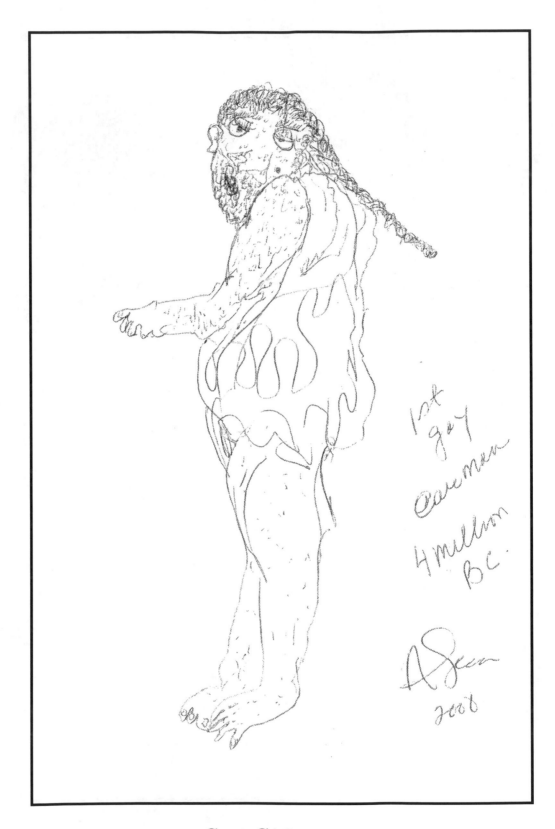

Gay Caveman

Ostrich Man

All Stars

Pointing at Pierre

A Gay In The French Foreign Legion

Walking To The Theater

Tolouse's Windswept Bride

A Feline's Ploy

Pyramid On Wheels Tour Guide

Stop The Mayhem

Dolente Carita

About the Author

Neil Baker is a novelist, short story writer, poet, artist, and a world renowned psychic. Neil also holds a degree in Psychology and has been a psychodramatist for a private psychiatric hospital. Neil has also managed a theater, candy store, golf store, All Night 7-11 and a motel. He has been a Child's Activities Director, Senior Director, gravedigger and Big Foot tracker and has accomplished this variety of roles while maintaing a somewhat questionable existence within the severe, physical contours of the earth.